CW01627303

DANGER – ENEMY ROBOT.

Earth has been invaded by the powerful robots from the distant planet Cybertron – the Heroic Autobots and their enemies, the Evil Decepticons. They can disguise their robot shapes as earthly machines and transform for battle at lightning speed. The battle between Good and Evil rages on Earth . . .

An exotic holiday island is terrorized by the murderous DIRGE. Brave BEACHCOMBER, a Heroic Autobot, needs your help to combat the Decepticon's menacing schemes. But the price of failure is death . . .

THE TRANSFORMERS™

ADVENTURE GAME BOOKS

Island of Fear

Also published by Young Corgi Books

THE TRANSFORMERS™: DINOBOT WAR
THE TRANSFORMERS™: PERIL FROM THE STARS
THE TRANSFORMERS™: HIGHWAY CLASH

THE TRANSFORMERS®

ADVENTURE GAME BOOKS

Island of Fear

Dave Morris
Illustrated by John Higgins

YOUNG CORGI BOOKS

THE TRANSFORMERS™:
ISLAND OF FEAR

A YOUNG CORGI BOOK 0 552 52316 X

PRINTING HISTORY
Young Corgi edition published 1986

© Hasbro Industries Inc. All rights reserved.
© text and illustrations Transworld Publishers Ltd.

Conditions of sale
1. This book is sold subject to the condition that it shall not, by way of trade *or otherwise*, be lent, re-sold, hired out or otherwise *circulated* without the publisher's prior consent in any form of binding or cover other than that in which it is published *and without a similar condition including this condition being imposed on the subsequent purchaser.*
2. This book is sold subject to the Standard Conditions of Sale of Net Books and may not be re-sold in the UK below the net price fixed by the publishers for the book.

Young Corgi Books are published by Transworld Publishers Ltd., 61–63 Uxbridge Road, Ealing, London W5 5SA.

Made and printed in Great Britain by the Guernsey Press Co. Ltd., Guernsey, Channel Islands.

This is an adventure story. But it is not like most other adventure stories – there is one big difference.

You are the main character.

What happens in the story depends on **your** decisions. The fate of The Transformers – whether the valiant Beachcomber will prevail or whether the evil schemes of DIRGE will succeed – is in your hands.

Do not read the pages of this adventure in numerical order, as you would an ordinary book. You should start at page **1**, of course, but where you go to from there will depend on what you choose to do.

Prepare yourself to meet The Transformers!

*NOW TURN TO PAGE **1** . . .*

Most people could never dream of having the chance to spend a whole summer vacationing on an island in the South Pacific. You are one of the lucky few, however, because your parents are two of the world's leading marine botanists. While they are off investigating the plants of a remote island chain, you are left to enjoy yourself in the unspoiled tropical paradise of Nali.

Today Akura, the islander who is looking after things in your parents' absence, has gone into the island's only large town to do some shopping. You sit on the patio and try to decide how you will spend the morning.

If you wish to go for a swim, turn to page **6**
If you decide to take a walk inland, turn to page **2**
If you get one of the islanders to take you out in his boat, turn to page **5**

You climb up to the rice terraces inland – stepped fields that descend down the sides of the hills of Nali Island. At this time in the morning, you would expect to see the islanders scattered about, hard at work in the rice fields. However, they are all huddled together in a large group by one of the irrigation ditches that pumps water to the fields.

If you decide to go and talk to them, turn to page **3**
If you would rather return to the beach, turn to page **4**

They do not speak very good English, but you hardly need to exchange more than a few words to see that they are all very frightened. Black muddy water is pouring down the ditch, polluting the rice fields. One of them points at the 'sacred' volcano in the centre of the island. 'Fire god angry!' he cries.

You tell them what your parents have told you – that the volcano is extinct. It has not erupted in thousands of years. You are not sure if they understand what you are saying or not.

Suddenly a distant rumbling echoes from the volcano!

Turn to page **9**

You slowly make your way back to the beach, wondering what the commotion in the rice fields was all about. You were thinking of getting one of the fishermen to take you out for a boat ride around the bay, but there are none in sight. It seems you will have to go for a swim after all.

Turn to page **6**

You go down to the beach and the islanders greet you in their usual friendly fashion. Mostly they are lazing about or repairing their boats. They will go fishing later in the day. A youth jumps up grinning as you point to his boat. You put out from the shore after offering him a few dollars. He is a skilled boatsman, and soon you are cutting gracefully through the clear blue waters of the bay.

Turn to page **10**

Going for a dip is a good idea – as usual, it is a hot day! Even the sea is luxuriously warm. You swim along the beach, occasionally treading water and calling out to the fishermen who are tending the nets on the white beach, until you reach the rocky point known locally as Rangda's Point.

Swimming further, you find a secluded cove you have visited once or twice before. It is a good place to go when you feel like doing nothing in particular, because it is quiet and private. As you run up from the frothy waves, you hear someone whistling. You are surprised – but the next moment you are completely astonished. Suddenly you see a robot come out from a nearby cave with a fishing rod over one shoulder!

Turn to page **8**

'Well, hey!' says the robot, almost as startled as you are yourself. 'How did you get here?'

'I swam,' you tell him. Then you start to smile – you can't help yourself. He looks rather funny holding the fishing rod.

'Oh yeah,' he replies, 'that's right, I forgot. You Earth-types float, don't you. I always wanted to try surfing . . .'

The thought of this big robot balanced on a surfboard makes you burst out laughing.

Turn to page **12**

The islanders shriek in terror at the sound. They seem unnecessarily frightened. Even if the volcano were to erupt – and you know that is impossible – it is a long way off and there is no immediate danger.

'Calm down!' you shout over the rumbling from the volcano. 'What's there to get so panicky about? It's just an earth tremor.'

As the rumbling dies down, they recover themselves. One of them turns to you. 'The voice of the god!' he declares, pointing to the volcano.

You shake your head, but they are firm in their superstitious ways. Leaving them, you return to the beach and take a swim.

Turn to page **6**

Suddenly the quiet peace of the bay is broken by a jet plane that comes screaming out from the centre of the island. You glance up as it blocks out the sun for a moment. It is a very unusual design of aeroplane, having two centrally mounted jets. You cannot help thinking that it is not very well designed, because it belches out a thick plume of black smoke as it flies. You watch as it completes a wide circle of the bay and flies back overhead, deafening you with the low roar of its engines. Strange – you didn't know there was an airstrip anywhere on Nali Island! Even stranger: when you turn to say something to the boatman, he is shaking with fear . . .

Turn to page **27**

The robot tells you that his name is BEACHCOMBER, and he is one of The Transformers – robots who came to Earth from the planet Cybertron millions of years ago. It is hard to believe, but since you find yourself talking to an intelligent robot – something you would have found incredible only a few minutes ago – you believe his amazing story.

Suddenly there is a screech of jet engines from high in the sky. You look up, but you cannot see a plane as it must be hidden behind the level of the clifftop. Glancing back at BEACHCOMBER, you are surprised to see that the noise has shaken him. As the sound of the jet fades into the distance, BEACHCOMBER asks you a strange thing. He asks you if you felt frightened.

If you say yes, turn to page **13**
If you tell him you're not frightened, turn to page **14**

'Sure!' you answer quickly. 'I was really scared.' You can't actually imagine what there was to be frightened about, but the noise of the jet obviously upset your robot friend.

'You didn't *look* very scared,' says BEACHCOMBER doubtfully.

'Oh, that's a thing with us humans. We don't show it when we're scared . . .'

'Really?' replies BEACHCOMBER. 'That's a new one to me. Still, I think I'd better tell you what that sound was –'

Turn to page **15**

You shrug. 'What was there to be frightened about? It was just a jet plane going over.'

'No, it wasn't!' exclaims BEACHCOMBER. 'But, wow, this is amazing – you must be one of the few people in the world who's immune to that sound. You know, just as some people are immune to chickenpox or metal fatigue or whatever –'

You are about to point out that no *person* you know ever suffered from metal fatigue, but BEACHCOMBER is about to explain about the jet . . .

Turn to page **15**

'The sound we heard can only have been DIRGE. He's one of the Evil Decepticons – a warlike group of robots that are trying to destroy the Autobots. I am one of the Autobots. DIRGE can transform himself into a jet plane, and the roar of his engines strikes terror into the fuel pumps of Transformers and humans alike!'

'Humans have hearts, not fuel pumps,' you put in.

'Very similar things. Anyway, if DIRGE is hanging out around here then some terrible plan is afoot. Much as I hate conflict, we must act before anyone is harmed.'

If you agree to help BEACHCOMBER, turn to page **16**
If you won't accompany him, turn to page **34**

BEACHCOMBER says that the first thing to do is discover where the evil DIRGE has his hideout. The two of you have to take the long route inland along the cliffs. Making your way down from the rocks, you trudge through the trees that line the shore. As you reach the beach, you spot an islander some distance away. He seems to be hiding and looks terrified.

If you call out to him, turn to page **18**
If you leave BEACHCOMBER here among the trees while you go and speak to the man, turn to page **19**

Hearing you shout, he looks up with surprise. The moment he catches sight of the pair of you standing among the trees, he cries with alarm and runs off. He runs straight into the sea and plunges through the waves, swimming quickly away with determined strokes.

'I think the sight of you must've frightened him off,' you say to BEACHCOMBER.

'For sure,' agrees BEACHCOMBER. 'Maybe he never saw a Transformer before. What do you think?'

'I think you're right. Which way shall we go now?'

If you walk along the beach, turn to page **22**
If you go inland, turn to page **23**

You walk up slowly and softly so as not to frighten the islander. Before you can ask him what happened to him, he starts to talk uncontrollably.

'An evil demon has come from the skies!' he cries. 'I myself saw him. It was Adurga, the Winged Messenger of Sorrow. The gods must be angry with us, and there is nothing we mortals can do.'

You have heard the islanders' legends and folklore. Adurga is their name for the Devil.

If you wish to rejoin BEACHCOMBER now, turn to page **21**

If you get the islander to tell you more, turn to page **20**

You ask the man where he saw the demon Adurga.

He looks about nervously as if expecting the demon to leap on his back at any moment. Then he cranes his neck up to whisper to you: 'He plunged through the skies like an arrow, capsizing our boats. I heard his evil laughter as he flew towards the sacred volcano –!'

He points to the towering cone of the volcano, several kilometres inland.

Turn to page **21**

You calm the man down before returning to where BEACHCOMBER is waiting for you among the trees. When you tell him what the islander saw, he nods his head grimly. 'That was no mere demon of myth,' he murmurs. 'It can only have been DIRGE.'

You stop to think for a moment, trying to decide where you should go from here. You could continue along the shoreline or else you could strike out inland.

If you continue along the beach, turn to page **22**
If you go inland from here, turn to page **23**

You continue along the white beach. Suddenly a deep rumbling fills the sky. DIRGE thunders overhead, trailing a plume of dirty black smoke. The sound makes BEACHCOMBER flinch, but he manages to control his misgivings. The treetops hide you from DIRGE's sight and he swoops off into the distance, out away from the island.

'I think he has his supplies and equipment on another island,' says BEACHCOMBER, 'and he's airlifting them to Nali for some evil purpose.'

'What is he up to?' you wonder. But BEACHCOMBER has no more idea than you do.

Turn to page **26**

You push your way through the thick undergrowth. You are far from the inhabited areas of the island, and the trails here are few and faint. Luckily, although BEACHCOMBER is not the toughest or the largest Autobot, he can easily beat a path for you. Above the treetops looms the dark grey cone of Mount Dorong, the 'sacred' volcano featured in the ancient myths of the island.

There is a snarl as something bulky comes crashing through the bushes. 'What—RAVAGE. . .?' says BEACHCOMBER uncertainly as you spy a catlike shape.

A tawny leopard appears only a few metres ahead of you, growling. There is a hungry gleam in its eyes. BEACHCOMBER stands his ground.

If you jump behind your friend, turn to page **25**
If you scramble up a nearby tree, turn to page **24**

You grab hold of a low-hanging branch and begin to climb up. Unfortunately, your quick movement attracts the leopard's attention – and it can climb trees as well! It leaps towards you, clearing the distance from the ground to your branch in one bound. BEACH-COMBER tries to catch it, but the leopard is too quick. Rather than describe the awful details of your fate, let us draw this story to an abrupt

END

The leopard leaps straight at BEACHCOMBER, roaring savagely as it does so. Thud! While it lies dazed from the impact with his metal chest, BEACHCOMBER reaches down and pinches a nerve in its neck. The leopard gives a startled grunt and blacks out. Soon it is purring in its sleep.

'Poor creature,' says BEACHCOMBER. 'It should stay unconscious until we can get back here and put it somewhere safe.'

'Strange,' you say. 'I didn't think there were any leopards on Nali Island.'

'There aren't. DIRGE must have brought it here to terrify any islanders who wander too close to his hideout. Like many bullies, DIRGE relies on fear as his main weapon. If fear fails, of course, he has several explosive missiles as a back-up . . .'

Having seen DIRGE, you know he is much larger and more powerful than your brave robot friend. How can the two of you hope to defeat him?

Turn to page **44**

You pass some planks of driftwood washed up on the shore. 'I like collecting things I find on beaches,' says BEACHCOMBER. 'It's always interesting to think where things like that came from – a wrecked fishing boat? A crate washed overboard in a storm? An old pirate galleon?' He laughs at the last idea. 'But I always seem to get drawn into the war against the Evil Decepticons. After four million years, you'd think both sides would know better . . .'

Coming to the end of the beach, you are faced with a high cliff. BEACHCOMBER suggests going inland from this point. You agree that DIRGE would not have his hideout on the shoreline.

You have gone only a few hundred metres when BEACHCOMBER gives a cry of shock. He has stumbled into a robot-trap – a tangle of cables which, coiled about his ankle, are sending thousands of volts through his body. He yells for you to get back, for he is too weak to free himself.

If you grab the cables and try to free your friend, turn to page **45**
If you try to pull him out of the snare of cables, turn to page **46**
If you run back to the beach, turn to page **47**

'Hey,' you tell the terrified boatman. 'It was only a jet plane.'

He stares at you, gasping for breath. 'Not only that,' he manages to say at last, shaking his head. 'Horrid noise, didn't you think?'

'No worse than Bangkok in the rush hour,' you reply with a laugh. 'Wow – what's *that*?'

Just entering the bay from the open sea is a shiny blue and yellow hovercraft.

If you hail it from your boat, turn to page **28**
If you ignore it and return to the shore, turn to page **37**

As far as you can tell, there is no-one steering the hovercraft. Nevertheless, as you call out it drifts to a halt beside your little boat. The boatman has recovered somewhat from his fright by now. He is as curious as you are, and begins to steer the boat closer to the hovercraft. But are you sure you want to investigate further?

If you tell him to take you back to the shore, turn to page **37**
If you go aboard the hovercraft, turn to page **29**

You go aboard the hovercraft but it is deserted.

'In that case,' says the boatman, who is right behind you, 'who was steering it?'

You cannot answer that, but you don't have to. Suddenly, a clear mechanical voice rings out: 'I was.'

Turn to page **30**

'Hello,' says the voice. 'I'm SEASPRAY.'

The image of a robot face appears on the computer console in front of you. You open your mouth to ask a dozen questions, but the robot starts talking first. 'I'm here,' he says. '*I'm* the hovercraft you're standing in. We Transformers are able to adopt the shape of Earth-vehicles, you see, and mine's a hovercraft. I'm sorry I can't appear to you in my true form but if I transformed now, we'd sink!'

'Well –' you begin to say, but your voice is drowned out by the screech of jet engines. The plane you saw earlier is returning. As it does, the image on the console begins to crackle. 'DIRGE!' SEASPRAY shouts 'Evil . . . Decepticon . . . M-must stop him . . .'

A surface-to-air laser appears from SEASPRAY's main hatch, but he seems to be unable to draw a bead on the approaching jet plane.

If you go out on deck to position the laser yourself, turn to page **32**
If you try to help by firing the laser from here, turn to page **33**

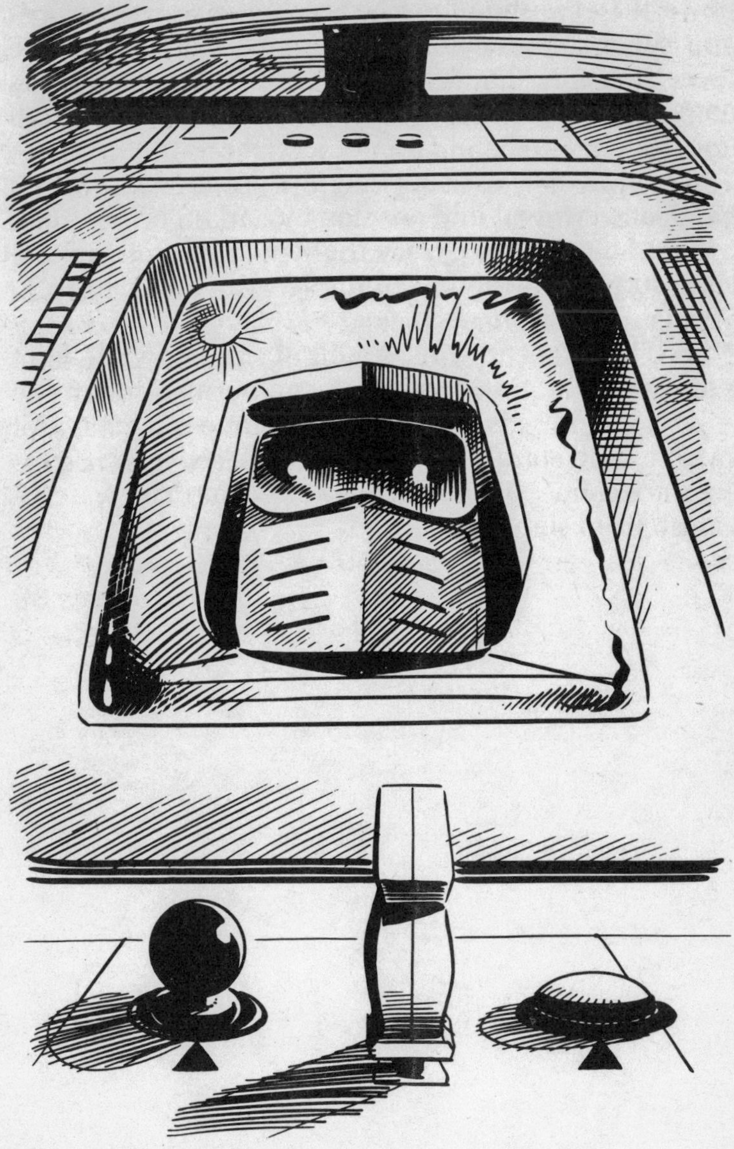

The boatman is also scared, but he struggles to master his fear as he comes out on to the deck with you. The powerful jet is shooting low across the water towards you, sunlight glinting off its deadly missiles. You realize there is something hypnotic about the sound of its engines. The sound causes terror in everyone, though you, for some reason, are not affected.

You grab the laser sticking out from SEASPRAY's hatch and swing it into position by hand. The boatman tries to help, but he is very frightened. As you aim the laser straight at the oncoming jet, you shout to SEASPRAY: 'Okay – *fire!*'

SEASPRAY hears you. A bolt of sizzling white light leaps from the tip of the laser and burns through the jet's wing. There is a snarl as if someone is in pain as it swerves and spirals back towards the shore. It is trailing smoke, but you did not get a direct hit. You watch it vanish from sight.

Turn to page **38**

You study the computer controls desperately. There may be a way to control the laser manually from here in the cabin – but which switch should you touch? You don't have much time. The jet plane is bearing down on you with ferocious speed, its missiles already primed.

If you press a green button, turn to page **35**
If you turn a yellow knob, turn to page **36**
If you try a blue joystick, turn to page **39**

Much as you would like to help BEACHCOMBER, you do not suppose there is much that you can do in a struggle between two robots. You tell him so, and he nods sadly. 'I'm afraid you're right,' he says. 'It is our fault that the Evil Decepticons are on Earth, in a way. I must stop DIRGE on my own.'

Casting away his fishing rod, he begins to clamber up the cliffs away from you. You wave and wish him luck, but he is too far away to hear you. You swim back to your villa. You will never know what an important part you might have played in today's adventure . . .

THE END

The hovercraft lurches as thrusters roar into life, sending you speeding through the water. You made a lucky guess – the jet plane's missiles strike the sea where you were floating just a moment ago. Fountains of spray rise into the air as they explode under the water. You are shaken but unharmed. The plane turns in the sky and returns to its base somewhere on the island.

Turn to page **38**

You twist the yellow knob, but all that happens is that you tune into a radio signal coming from the attacking jet. A horrible voice crackles from the radio loudspeaker: 'Fear is the element that unites all losers. Farewell, SEASPRAY . . .'

Missiles streak from the jet straight towards you. There is no time to do anything else. You screw your eyes tight shut. This is

THE END

Still wondering about the strange hovercraft, you return to the beach. The other fishermen are all talking excitedly about the mysterious jet plane you saw earlier. Your boatman begins to tell a story about having seen it close up. As you cannot understand the islanders' language, you walk away. You cannot understand why the sight or the sound of the plane should give them all such a scare. They must have seen seaplanes before now.

You decide to take a walk inland and see if you can find the plane's airstrip.

Turn to page **2**

As the awful roar of the jet's engines fades into the distance, SEASPRAY and the boatman recover.

'I think I'd better explain, says The Transformer. 'That was no ordinary plane – it was DIRGE, one of the Evil Decepticons. I tracked him with my radar and I believe he has a base on this island. It is very important that we find one of the Heroic Autobots, BEACHCOMBER, who is vacationing around here somewhere. He likes to be alone. Is there anywhere private around here where you wouldn't be disturbed?'

As a matter of fact there is. You have visited a small secluded cove some distance along the shore. BEACHCOMBER could be there . . . but do you want to tell SEASPRAY about that?

If you tell him, turn to page **40**
If you keep it to yourself, turn to page **41**

As you move the joystick, SEASPRAY's terrified face disappears from the console to be replaced by a computer display of the oncoming jet. A small light moves across the screen as you operate the joystick. This is rather fun, you think to yourself – like playing an arcade game! The light shows where SEASPRAY's laser is pointing. As soon as you have the jet square in your sights you press the fire button. A thin streak of white laser-light burns up through the jet's wing. It turns off and flies back towards the island, damaged but still airborne.

Turn to page **38**

You tell SEASPRAY about the cove. 'It sounds just the sort of place BEACHCOMBER likes,' he agrees. He starts up his motors and you guide him along the coast to where the cove lies, just beyond Rangda's Point.

As you round the line of the coast, you spy a metallic figure perched on a large flat rock. He seems to be fishing. 'BEACHCOMBER!' calls out SEASPRAY.

The robot looks up. 'Go away, SEASPRAY,' he replies. 'I'm on holiday.'

'Decepticons don't take holidays,' replies SEASPRAY as he drifts closer to the shore. 'There's one on this very island. It's DIRGE, and you can bet he's planning something evil.'

BEACHCOMBER throws down his fishing rod. 'Oh, well,' he sighs, 'I hadn't caught anything anyway.' That doesn't surprise you; as you leap ashore, you notice he was using a rusty iron bolt for bait!

Turn to page **42**

BEACHCOMBER could be staying at the cove, but you decide that you don't wish to get involved with these strange alien robots. 'I can't think of anywhere,' you tell SEASPRAY. 'Have you tried Taulo Island? It's only a few kilometres away.'

'I shall go there now,' he replies. After you and the islander have returned to the fishing boat, SEASPRAY turns around and motors out of the bay. You watch him go, wondering whether you made the right decision. How would things have gone if you had helped him find BEACHCOMBER? You may find out if you start the adventure again from page 1, but for now this is

THE END

'Who're you?' asks BEACHCOMBER.

'This is a friend of mine, very willing to help in the fight against DIRGE,' says SEASPRAY before you can reply.

'I don't like fighting, SEASPRAY. You know that,' announces BEACHCOMBER.

'No choice. My robot-form isn't mobile enough to go clambering about the jungles and hills of this island, and there's no time to summon the other Autobots. You and the kid will have to do the job between you.'

'Great!' BEACHCOMBER gives a short, unamused laugh. 'DIRGE is outnumbered two-to-one; he'll probably just surrender . . .'

BEACHCOMBER doesn't think you'll be of much help against the Decepticon, but SEASPRAY corrects him. He has seen that you're immune to the petrifying fright of DIRGE's battle-roar. BEACHCOMBER is impressed.

Turn to page **43**

SEASPRAY cannot come any further with you. He wishes the two of you luck, then turns to take the boatman back to the beach. With BEACHCOMBER at your side, you set out on your adventure. Making your way along the rocky fringe around Rangda's Point, you head through the trees that line the shore. After a few minutes you spot an islander crouched on the beach. He appears to have had a severe fright, because he is trembling with his hands over his head.

If you call out to him, turn to page **18**
If you leave BEACHCOMBER waiting here among the trees while you go and speak to the islander, turn to page **19**

You continue at a brisk pace. The 'sacred' volcano looms ahead of you, and by mid-afternoon you have reached its lower slopes. The sun is high in the sky and the air is hot and dusty here. Suddenly DIRGE roars through the heavens overhead, having taken off right out of the cone of the volcano. Controlling the fear that his enemy's screaming jets cause, BEACHCOMBER pulls you back behind a rock. DIRGE fails to notice you, and sweeps across the island towards the sea.

Turn to page **49**

You bravely seize one of the cables that is caught around BEACHCOMBER's ankle. Unfortunately, this only causes thousands of volts to pass through *your* body as well. You are not as tough as BEACHCOMBER – his circuits are beginning to dangerously overheat, but you don't have time to feel a thing before you meet your

END

BEACHCOMBER is weakening fast. You take hold of his arm, intending to pull him away from the electrified cable. But you have forgotten that, being metal, BEACHCOMBER's body conducts electricity! A deadly shocks sears through your body, and you pass out never to recover.

THE END

Knowing how dangerous electricity can be, you rush back to the beach. Choosing the sturdiest plank you can find amid the driftwood you saw earlier, you hurry back to BEACHCOMBER's side. He is almost unconscious with pain. Hastily you push the cables away from him with the insulating wooden plank. While he recovers, you push the bushes aside with your plank. The cables all run into a generator that was hidden there. You smash it with a rock so that no islanders will stumble into this merciless trap.

Turn to page **48**

'That's another use for driftwood,' you tell BEACH-COMBER.

'Thank you, my friend,' he answers, getting to his feet now that his strength is returning. 'DIRGE must have planted that trap, and I would have died in it if not for your quick thinking.' You feel very proud!

Continuing at a good pace, you are approaching the dusty slopes of the island's volcano by mid-afternoon. Something tells you that DIRGE's hideout is nearby now.

Turn to page **49**

Clambering up the steep lava slopes of the volcano looks like it might be exhausting work, but BEACH-COMBER says it will not be a problem. He begins to shift his shape, and quickly becomes a smart beach buggy with large tyres. 'I can handle some pretty difficult terrain in this form,' he says. 'Hop in and hold tight!'

BEACHCOMBER carries you quickly up the side of the volcano, throwing up clouds of black ash from his rugged tyres. You are soon at the lip of the crater.

'I've been using my sensors to measure what's going on in the ground below us,' says BEACHCOMBER as he returns to his Autobot form. 'DIRGE has been meddling with some heavy equipment inside the volcano. He's probably been drilling down into the Earth's crust. If he isn't stopped he could release a torrent of molten rock that could destroy the entire island!'

Does BEACHCOMBER know that you are immune to DIRGE's fear-creating soundwaves?

If he has been told this, turn to page **50**
If he doesn't know it, turn to page **51**

'Normally I wouldn't put you in any danger,' says BEACHCOMBER. 'But many lives are at stake, and your immunity to DIRGE's power makes you a valuable companion. Are you willing to enter his hideout with me?'

You are afraid, but you cannot back out now. You nod in agreement, and the two of you walk down into the volcano's crater. An open steel door sticks out through the heavy black ash. It is the entrance to DIRGE's headquarters. With barely a moment's hesitation, you step inside . . .

Turn to page **55**

'It's best if you wait here,' says BEACHCOMBER. 'It may be dangerous. I'll take a look round then come back for you.' Before you can protest, he edges himself down inside the rim of the volcano. Sticking out from the cold ash you can see a shining steel door – the entrance to DIRGE's hideaway! With a last wave to you, BEACHCOMBER vanishes inside.

You wait anxiously for several minutes. Becoming aware of a low droning in the air, you turn to see DIRGE streaking back towards his hideout. In another moment he may spot you! Do you crouch down where you are, or break from cover and run to join BEACHCOMBER inside the hideout?

If you stay where you are, turn to page **52**
If you enter the hideout, turn to page **54**

You hide behind a rock, not daring to move a muscle in case DIRGE should see you. Landing beside the hideout door, he turns back to his robot form. He is a much larger and obviously stronger robot than BEACHCOMBER. He steps within and an instant later, the door closes.

You scramble down, but you can see no way to get it open again from this side. You wait beside the door for hours, praying that BEACHCOMBER will outwit the Evil Decepticon or at least find some way to escape from him. It is after dark when you finally return home, having seen no sign of the Heroic Autobot. Some dreadful fate has surely befallen him – and who now can save Nali Island from DIRGE's evil plans? You can think of no-one.

THE END

70

You see no other way to warn BEACHCOMBER, even though there is a danger that DIRGE will see you. You break from cover and scramble down into the volcanic crater, hurling yourself through the open doorway an instant before DIRGE passes overhead. You hurry along the corridor and soon catch up with your friend.

Turn to page **55**

As you walk along a winding corridor that goes right down into the depths of the inactive volcano, BEACHCOMBER suddenly holds up a hand to stop you. 'Look up there,' he whispers, pointing. You see a crystal rod wound with copper wire. 'It's an electronic jammer, designed to send instruments haywire. If I'd gone any closer it would've scrambled my circuits!'

Turn to page **56**

'DIRGE obviously only expected other robots to break into his hideout,' you say. Stepping over to the jammer, you take it down from the wall and put it in your pocket. You signal 'OK' to BEACHCOMBER and he hurries to join you.

Turn to page **57**

'My sensors are picking up something nearby,' he says in a worried voice, 'but I can't pinpoint it. It's as though something invisible were following us –'

Then he falls silent, because you have reached the nerve centre of DIRGE's underground lair!

Turn to page **58**

You and BEACHCOMBER are standing on a high walkway above DIRGE's control room. DIRGE himself is busy on the floor below you, tending to various instrument panels. 'He must have entered by another route,' you whisper, pointing to a large hangar door on the far side of the room.

BEACHCOMBER's attention is on a huge laser attached to the walkway beside you. 'This is what he's using to drill down into the Earth,' he murmurs. 'He must be trying to tap the power of the Earth's core to fuel the Decepticons' weapons!'

If you think you should use the laser to shoot DIRGE from above, turn to page **65**
If you wait here until DIRGE leaves, turn to page **59**

You wait in dead silence, watching as DIRGE checks the readings on his computer displays far below. At last he is ready to leave, probably to collect more equipment and supplies. He presses a button and the hangar doors slide back with a rumbling sound. DIRGE's body reshapes itself into the ominous jet fighter you saw earlier. Then he screeches away into the open sky. The hangar doors close by themselves.

'Now we can wreck some of his equipment,' you say to BEACHCOMBER. 'He won't be back for a while.'

BEACHCOMBER does not reply. When you turn to see why, you find he has taken hold of the massive laser and swung it to point along the walkway – straight at you! Is he going to shoot you? Will you:

Stand right where you are? Turn to page **60**
Dodge to one side? Turn to page **62**
Activate the electronic jammer? Turn to page **63**

You stand completely motionless, knowing that your friend would never do a thing to harm you. You are right – he is aiming at a hideous gooey monster that is slithering up behind you. You feel one of its soft tentacles touch your ankle, making your skin crawl. Then BEACHCOMBER unleashes a sparkling bolt from the laser and the creature shrivels up. Soon all that is left of it is a sticky yellow puddle and a thick, nasty smoke in the air.

Turn to page **61**

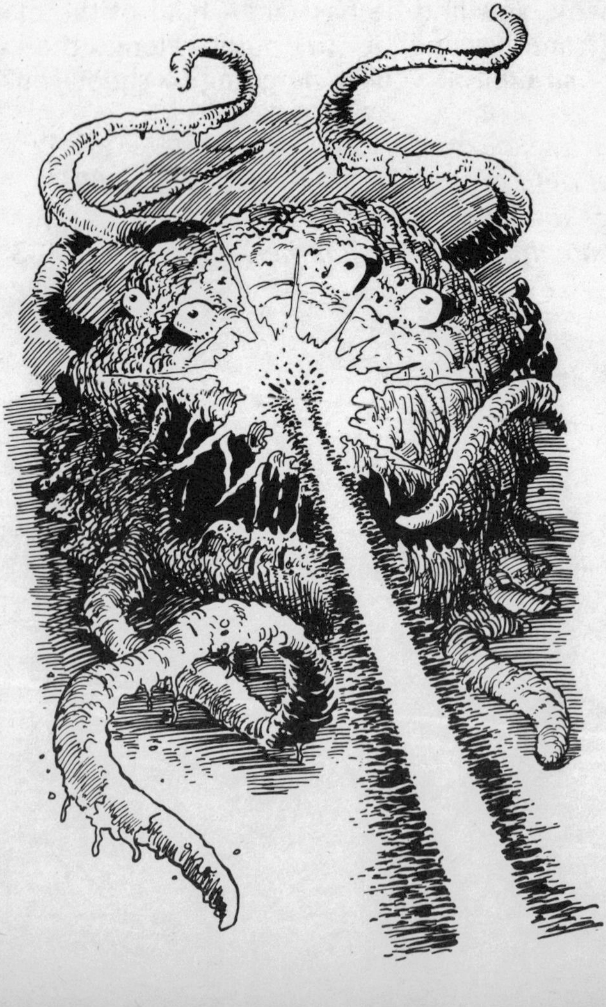

'Phew!' says BEACHCOMBER. 'Sorry if I gave you a fright just then, but I saw that monster crawling up on you while DIRGE was still here. I couldn't call out a warning without attracting his attention.'

'What on earth *was* it?' you ask, looking at the oily puddle.

'Nothing from Earth, in fact. It's Denebian Stalker – comes from another planet. DIRGE must've brought this one to Earth as a pet, would you believe.'

'That must be what you detected on your sensors earlier,' you say. 'It's been following us in the shadows since we entered . . . Yuck!'

If you now suggest that BEACHCOMBER smashes the computer controls, turn to page **66**
If you think it would be wiser to hide the electronic jammer inside DIRGE's laser and then leave, turn to page **64**

You throw yourself to one side as BEACHCOMBER touches the fire button. You should have trusted him – he wasn't firing at you, but at something just behind you. Unfortunately you stepped right into the path of his carefully aimed laser beam. The last thing you ever hear is BEACHCOMBER calling out your name, horrified that he has shot his own friend by accident.

THE END

'Hey, I don't know what's got into you, BEACH-COMBER, but I don't want to be burned to a cinder!' You take the jammer from your pocket and point it at the laser in his hands. Sparks fly from the laser as your jammer causes it to backfire. BEACHCOMBER topples from the walkway stunned, but you have no time to worry about him. An alien creature made of gooey jelly oozes over you from behind. BEACHCOMBER was not about to shoot you at all – he was about to destroy this hideous alien that was creeping up on you! It is too late to think about that now. The alien is enjoying you as its main meal of the day. The most you can hope is that you will give it indigestion!

THE END

You wedge the jammer inside the huge laser. 'There. The next time DIRGE tries to use this to drill into the Earth's crust, he's in for a nasty shock.'

But there is no time left. The hangar doors are beginning to swing open automatically. DIRGE is returning! You and BEACHCOMBER hurry out along the corridor to the other doorway.

As you go down the slopes of the volcano, you hear a deafening explosion from below your feet. The ground starts to tremble, and BEACHCOMBER turns into his car-form to rush you to safety as the volcano starts to erupt!

'The exploding laser must've set off a chain reaction,' says BEACHCOMBER as you watch the eruption from a distance. 'We stopped DIRGE's evil plan, but the volcanic ash will ruin the islanders' crops . . .'

'Hey, look on the bright side,' you tell him. 'Better to lose their crops than to lose their lives!'

THE END

BEACHCOMBER refuses. 'It would be too dangerous,' he says sternly. 'It might cause a volcanic eruption. Wait, and we will find a peaceful solution to this problem.'

You don't think that's very likely. With the lives of thousands of islanders at stake, you decide that you must act now. Slipping past BEACHCOMBER, you click the switch on the side of the laser before he can stop you. A brilliant beam of light stabs down. By a stroke of good luck it strikes DIRGE, and he screams in rage and pain. By a stroke of bad luck, however, it also strikes some instruments behind him. A chain reaction is set off within moments, and you, BEACHCOMBER and the entire hideout are burnt to a crisp in a single titanic explosion!

THE END

BEACHCOMBER starts smashing the instrument panels, quickly shattering all the equipment which DIRGE has been using for his evil plans. Lastly he deals with the huge drilling laser, breaking the ruby rod inside it with a chop of his metal hand. A shower of sparks rises from the wreckage.

The two of you hurry from the hideout just as a black shadow blots out the sun. It is DIRGE. 'What are you doing here?' he thunders, hovering above you. 'Prepare to die for your meddling, fools!'

He is about to release his deadly missiles when you take out the electronic jammer and point it at him. DIRGE shudders and lifts further into the air. 'See how you like a taste of your own medicine,' you tell him. 'Leave this island right now. I intend to give this device of yours to the islanders. If you ever return to bother them, they will use it to destroy you!'

'N-no!' cries DIRGE, retreating further into the sky. 'I'll go!' He streaks off into the evening sun.

'Looks like we did okay, huh?' you say to BEACHCOMBER. 'Want to spend the rest of your holidays at my place while my parents are away?'

'That,' replies BEACHCOMBER, 'would be really *cool*!'

THE END

THE TRANSFORMERS™: DINOBOT WAR
by Dave Morris

Robot Dinosaurs!

Earth has been invaded by the powerful robots from the distant plant Cybertron – the Heroic Autobots and their enemies, the Evil Decepticons. They can disguise their robot shapes as earthly machines and transform for battle at lightning speed. The battle between Good and Evil rages on Earth . . .

You are the hero of this book – suddenly you are thrust into the deadly struggle. With the help of secret devices, found on an ancient flying saucer, you could travel back to prehistoric times and help the Heroic Dinobots in their battle against the Evil Decepticons.

If you dare . . .

If you collect Transformers™, this book is for you!

SBN 0 0552 523143

THE TRANSFORMERS™
PERIL FROM THE STARS
by Dave Morris

Evil Robots walk among us!

Earth has been invaded by the powerful robots from the distant planet Cybertron – the Heroic Autobots and their enemies, the Evil Decepticons. They can disguise their robot shapes as earthly machines and transform for battle at lightning speed. The battle between Good and Evil rages on Earth . . .

You are the hero of this book – suddenly you are thrust into the deadly struggle

You will meet the valiant Autobot JAZZ and help him fight against the evil STARSCREAM. But be careful – your actions will decide whether the Decepticon is defeated or whether he gets the terrible weapons he needs to overthrow the world!

If you collect Transformers™, this book is for you!

SBN 0 552 523151

T.R. BEAR: ENTER T.R.
by Terrance Dicks

It all started when Jimmy got a parcel from his Uncle Colin in America. The teddy bear inside was unlike any bear Jimmy had ever seen. He looked tough, and he was wearing glasses! According to the label, his name was Theodore Roosevelt, T.R. for short.

Jimmy soon found out that life with T.R. Bear was quite eventful . . .

SBN 0 552 523011

If you would like to receive a newsletter telling you about our new children's books, fill in the coupon with your name and address and send it to:

The Children's Books Editor,
Transworld Publishers Ltd.,
61–63 Uxbridge Road, Ealing,
London, W5 5SA

Name ....

Address ....

....

....

CHILDREN'S NEWSLETTER

All the books on the previous pages are available at your bookshop or can be ordered direct from Transworld Publishers Ltd., Cash Sales Dept., P.O. Box 11, Falmouth, Cornwall.
Please send full name and address together with cheque or postal order — no currency, and allow 55p per book to cover postage and packing (plus 22p each for additional copies).